GRANDPA Kevin's

really kinda strange, somewhat bizarre and overly unrealistic...

ABC

BOOK

by Kevin J. Brougher & Lisa M. Brougher

Missing Piece Press, LLC

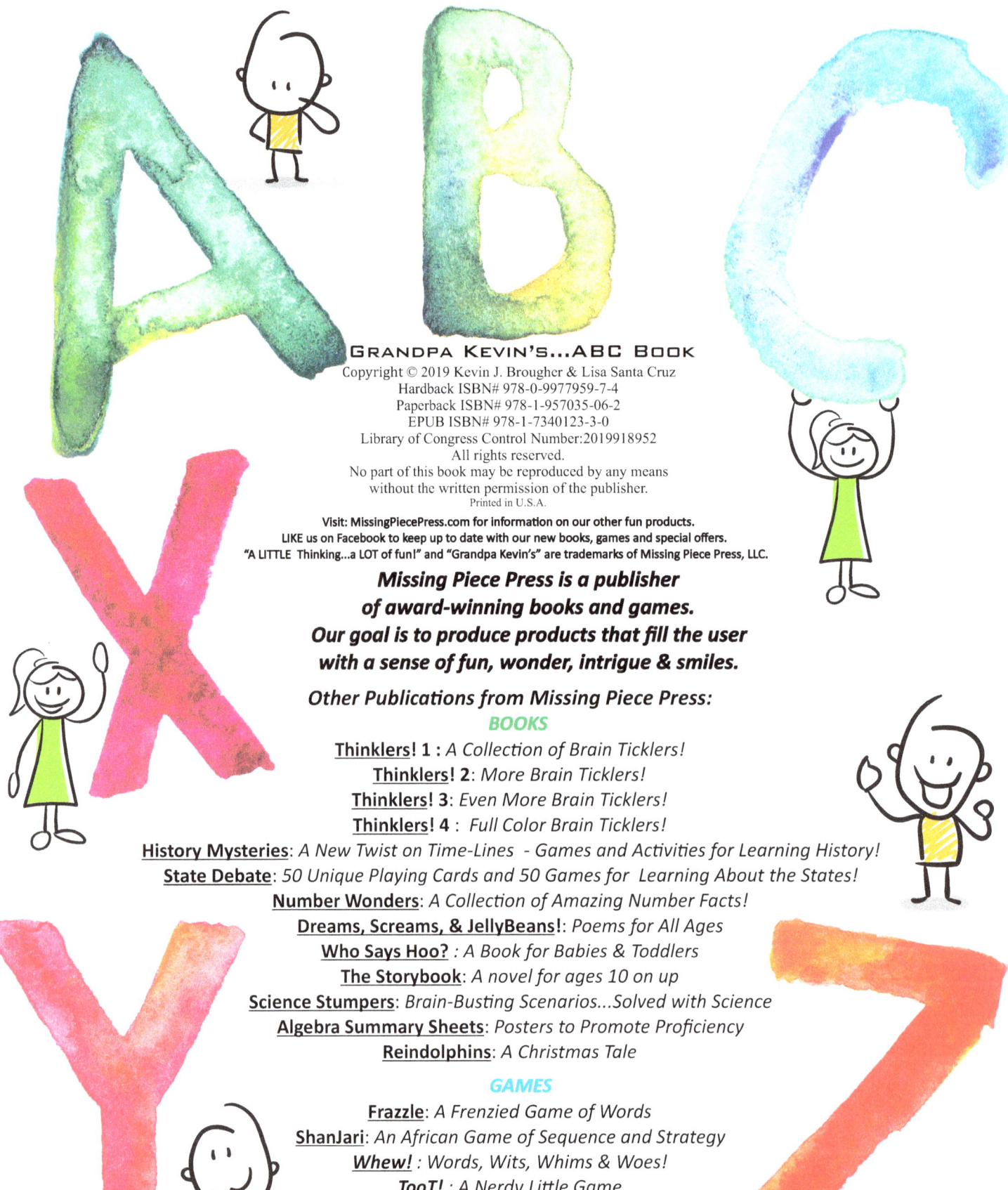

Grandpa Kevin's...ABC Book
Copyright © 2019 Kevin J. Brougher & Lisa Santa Cruz
Hardback ISBN# 978-0-9977959-7-4
Paperback ISBN# 978-1-957035-06-2
EPUB ISBN# 978-1-7340123-3-0
Library of Congress Control Number:2019918952
All rights reserved.
No part of this book may be reproduced by any means
without the written permission of the publisher.
Printed in U.S.A.

Visit: MissingPiecePress.com for information on our other fun products.
LIKE us on Facebook to keep up to date with our new books, games and special offers.
"A LITTLE Thinking...a LOT of fun!" and "Grandpa Kevin's" are trademarks of Missing Piece Press, LLC.

**Missing Piece Press is a publisher
of award-winning books and games.
Our goal is to produce products that fill the user
with a sense of fun, wonder, intrigue & smiles.**

Other Publications from Missing Piece Press:

BOOKS

Thinklers! 1 : *A Collection of Brain Ticklers!*
Thinklers! 2: *More Brain Ticklers!*
Thinklers! 3: *Even More Brain Ticklers!*
Thinklers! 4 : *Full Color Brain Ticklers!*
History Mysteries: *A New Twist on Time-Lines - Games and Activities for Learning History!*
State Debate: *50 Unique Playing Cards and 50 Games for Learning About the States!*
Number Wonders: *A Collection of Amazing Number Facts!*
Dreams, Screams, & JellyBeans!: *Poems for All Ages*
Who Says Hoo? : *A Book for Babies & Toddlers*
The Storybook: *A novel for ages 10 on up*
Science Stumpers: *Brain-Busting Scenarios...Solved with Science*
Algebra Summary Sheets: *Posters to Promote Proficiency*
Reindolphins: *A Christmas Tale*

GAMES

Frazzle: *A Frenzied Game of Words*
ShanJari: *An African Game of Sequence and Strategy*
Whew! : *Words, Wits, Whims & Woes!*
TooT! : *A Nerdy Little Game*
Blam! : *A Different Card Game*
DICE Blam! : *A Different Dice Game*
Word Nerd : *A Quick-Witted Word Game*
Bunco BUDDIES! : *The BETTER Bunco Game*
CRUMMY : *The Criss-Cross Rummy Game*
Take 12 : *The Token Taking Game*
...and more! **MissingPiecePress.com**

For the Santa Cruz TWINS - who are surely the smartest two boys the world has ever seen and who will undoubtedly learn ALL the words in this book, most likely, after just the first reading.

For the rest of you...you should probably read this to your kids and grandkids MANY MANY times.

A is for ADVENTURESOMENESS

ad-**ven**-cher-suhm-nes

Willing to take risks.

...a rambling word!
It's long. It's weird.
It's almost absurd!
But, if A is the letter,
a good place to start
is **APPLE**,

ANT,

APE

and **ART**!

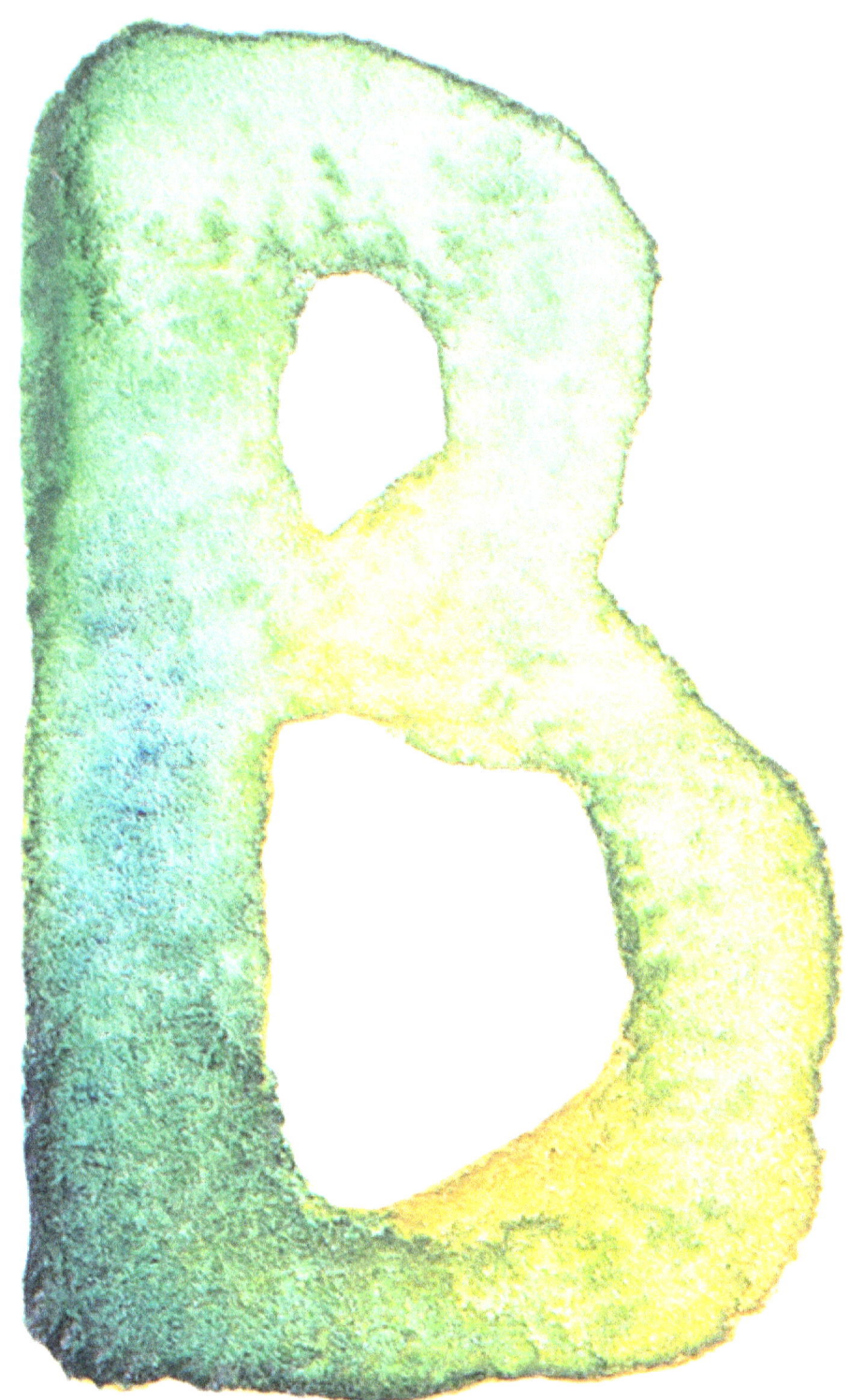

is for
BUREAUCRATIZATION.
byoo-*rok*-ruh-tahy-zay-shun
Forming or converting of something into a government run (or similar) system.

How scary is that?

Other  words are...

BAGELS

and BAT.

Or, BUTTERFLY,

BOAT,

BOOKS

or BERRY.

But, BUREAUCRATIZATION...
is downright scary!

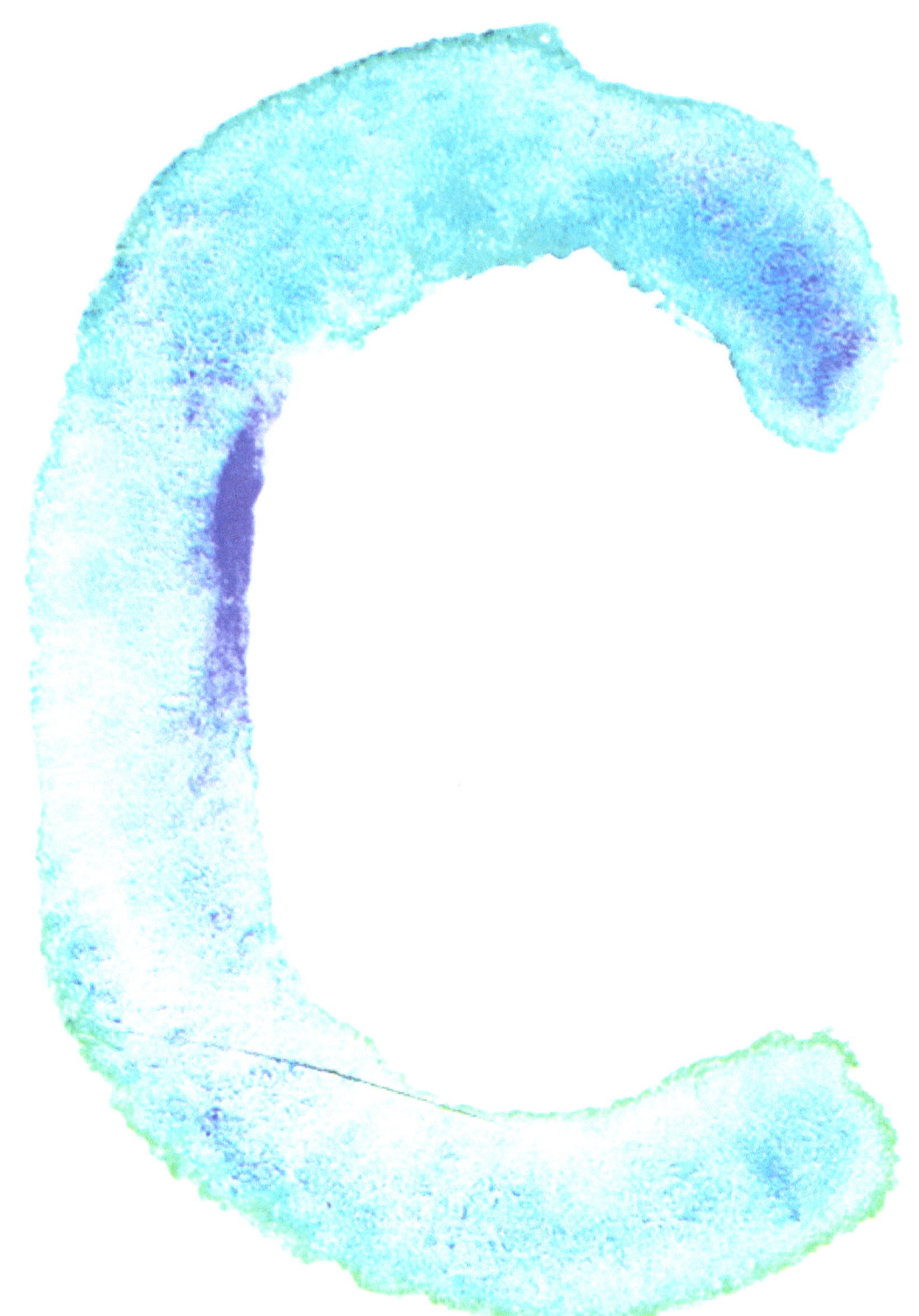

C is for CONCEPTUALIZATION.

kuhn-sep-choo-uh-lahy-zay-shun

An abstract idea of something.

That's bigger than CAT.

It's bigger than CHAIR.

It's bigger than CHAT.

It's longer than CRAYONS.

It's longer than COW.

Some can pronounce it.
Do **you** know how?

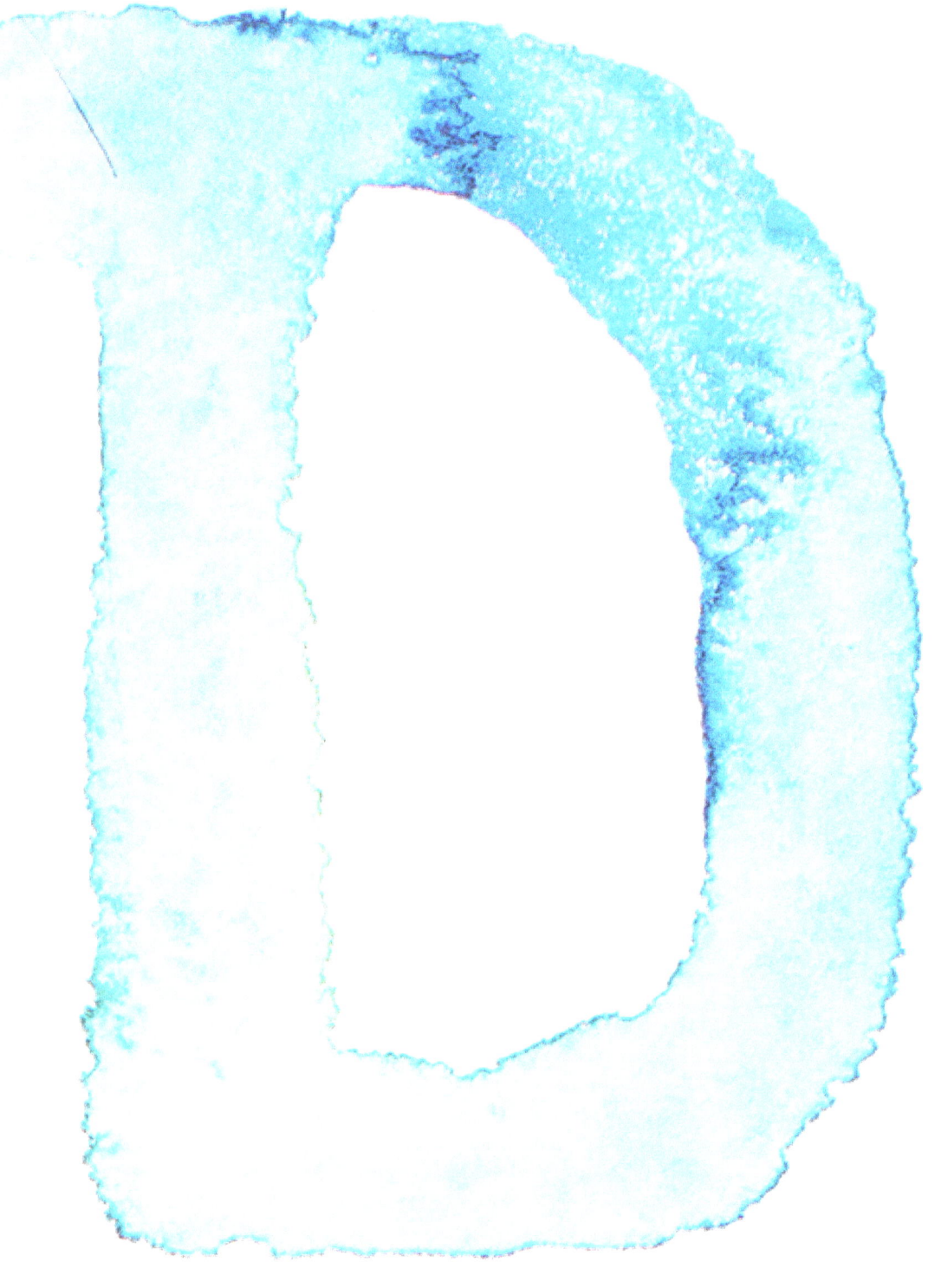

D is for DISCOMBOBULATING.

dis-kuhm-*bob*-yuh-lay-ting

To confuse, frustrate or upset.

That's funny and long!
I'd love to hear it - sung in a song.

Other words are DOG

and DOOR,

DAD

or DESERT,

DICE

and DRAWER.

E is for EXTRAORDINARINESS.

ek-*strawr*-din-er-ee-nes
That which is beyond the usual or ordinary.

E is also for EAR.

It's the beginning of EGG

and, yes, ENGINEER.

It's also for ELEPHANT - with big round feet.

To get **THAT** big - they Eat - Eat - Eat!

F is for FORETHOUGHTFULNESS –

fohr-*thawt*-fuhl-nes

An act of thinking ahead.

a nice but, long word!

One, that I doubt, you ever have heard.

F's also for **FROG**,

FLOWER

and **FISH**.

There are **MANY** more.

Look them up - if you wish.

is for
GREATHEARTEDNESS
greyt-*hahr*-tid-nes
The act of showing kindness, love and compassion.

- a good word to know.

So is GAME,

GRAPES

or GROW!

There's also GIRAFFE,

GREAT and GOOD.

Learn them all - I think you should.

H is for HONORIFICABILITUDINITATIBUS.

on-uh-***rif***-ik-uh-bil-uh-tewd-ih-nih-tat-ih-bus

The state of being able to achieve honors.

Wow! A mouthful for sure.

But, other H words are

HIS  or  HER.

There's also HOT

and HORSE,

and HAY.

Learn them all - is what I say.

is for
INCOMPREHENSIBILITY
in-kom-pri-hen-suh-*bil*-uh-tee
That which is not able to be understood, or is not intelligible.

But, you know what I think?

Some easier words are

IGLOO

and INK.

There's also ICE,

ITCH

and IGUANA.

Learn them all – if you wanna.

is for JUSTIFIABLENESSES

juhs-tuh-*fahy*-uh-buhl-nes
The ability of something to be justified.

It's a good word and yet,

it's easier to say : JUG,

JAM

or JET.

Other  words are JELLY

or JAR -  JUMP

and JACKET

or even... JAGUAR.

is for
KNOWLEDGEABLENESS
nol-i-juh-buhl-nes
A persons understanding of something.

K is also for **KEY**,

It starts KOALA.

It starts KIWI.

K is for KITE.

It starts KANGAROO -

KETCHUP

and KING -

to name just a few.

is for
LACKADAISICALLY

lak-uh-*dey*-zik-lee

Done without enthusiasm.

It's starts the word LUNCH.

It begins the word LOG.

There's more - there's a bunch!

Like LION

and LEAF

and LEMONS

and LIMES.

You're learning them now

with these words that rhyme.

M is for MISCHARACTERIZATIONS

mis-*kar*-ik-tuh-rahyz-ay-shuns
More than one incorrect attempts at identifying a character trait.

That's a **MOUTHFUL** to say.

What's easier said,

is the **MONTH** of **MAY**.

Or, **MILK**

or **MOON**   or **MOM**

or **MOUSE**.

Or, maybe, **MUD**

...that's tracked into the house.

is for
NONRELATIVISTICALLY
non-rel-uh-tuh-*vis*-tik-lee
Not relating to relativism.

THAT's hard to recite!

Easier words are NOODLES

or NIGHT.

There's also NAP

and NUMBERS 1 2 3 4 ...

and NET.

For your first N words -
You've got 'em - you're set!

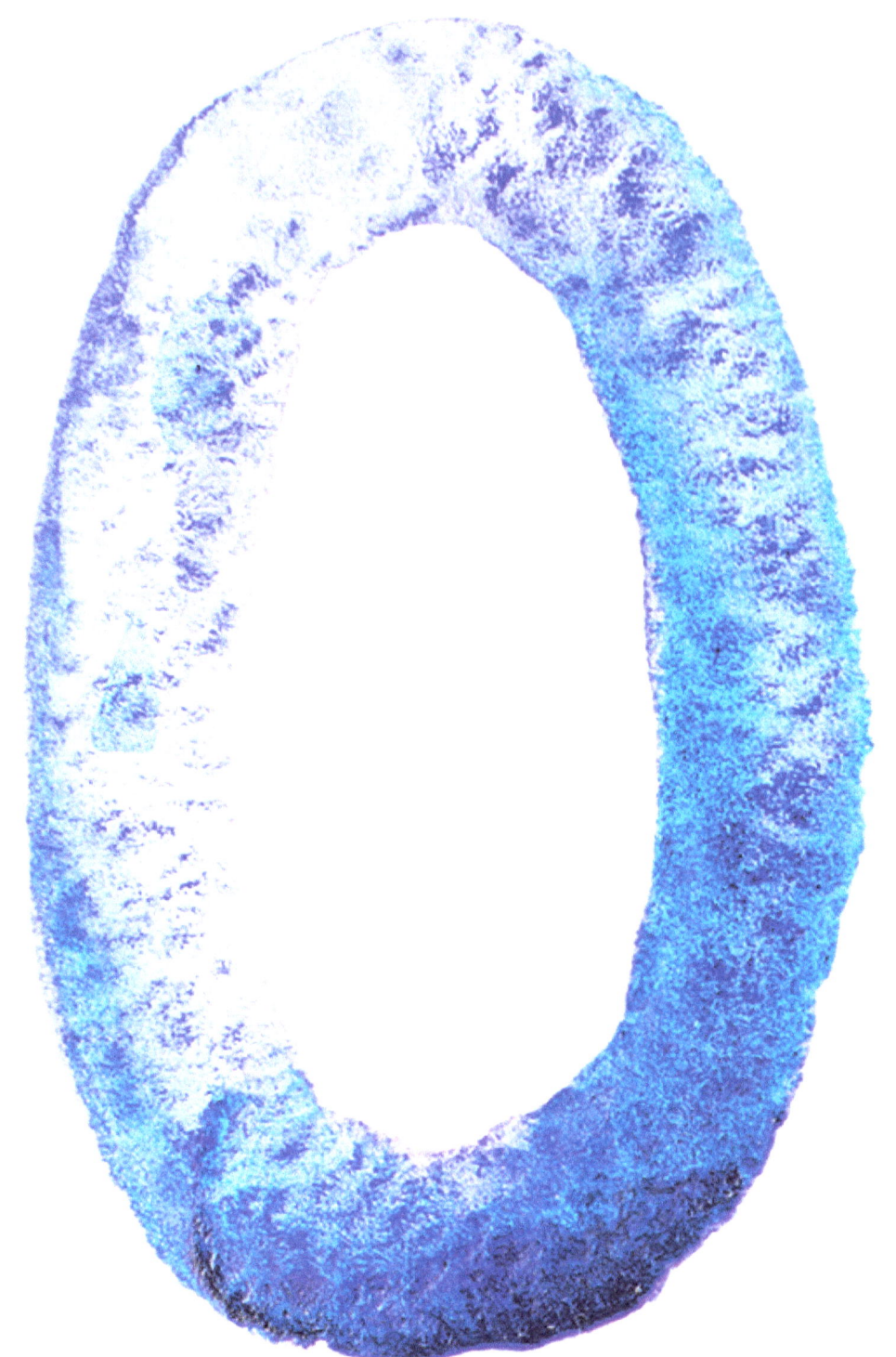

O is for OVERINTELLECTUALIZATIONS

o-ver-in-tl-*ek*-choo-uh-lahy-zay-shuns

Many attempts at making something more rational or logical.

That can make a tongue toil!

So, start with OX

or OSTRICH

or OIL.

Of course, there is OVAL,

ONIONS

and ONE.

Learning  words is OBSESSIVELY fun!

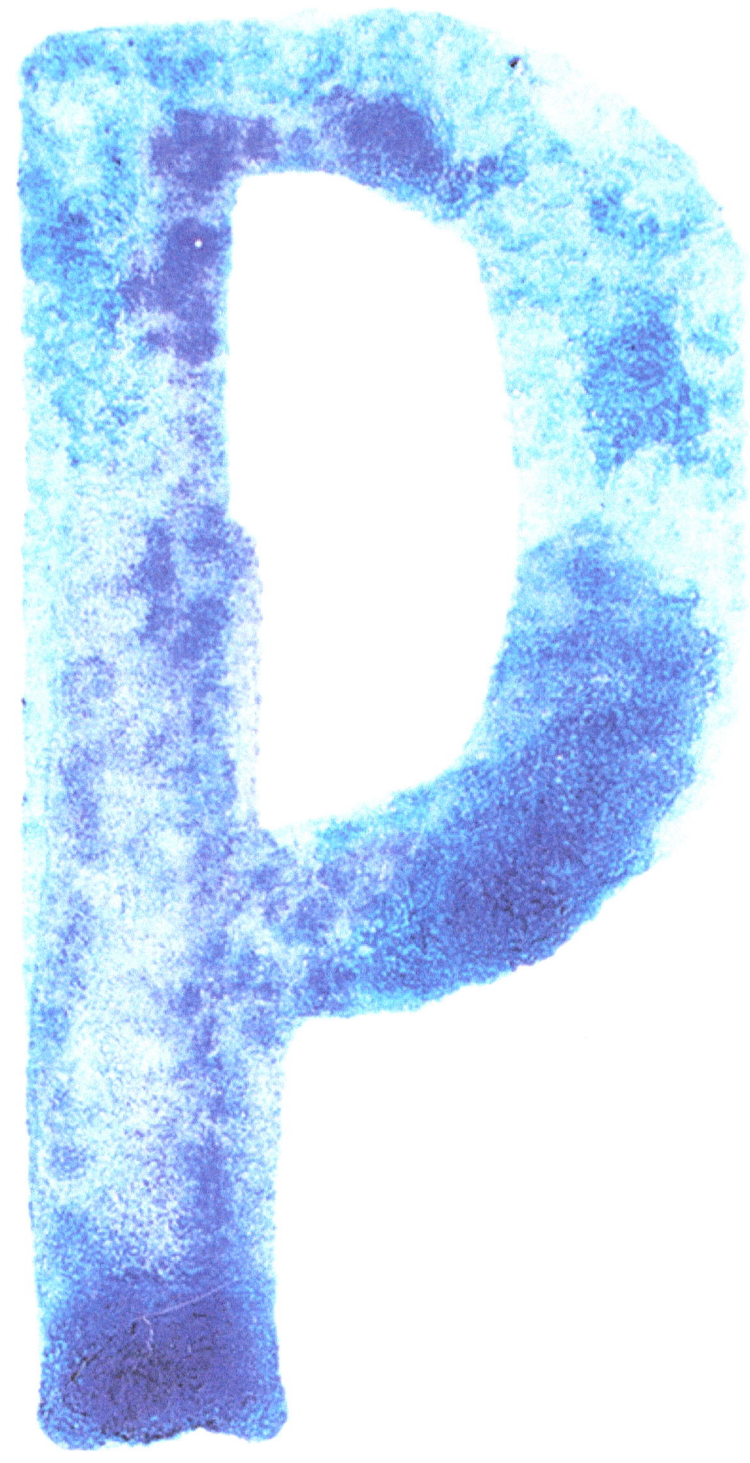

P is for PREPOSTEROUSNESS

pri-**pos**-ter-uhs-nes

The stupidness, foolishness or ridiculousness of something.

That word's long as can be!

A shorter  word is PICKLE

or PEA.

Or, PET

or PENGUIN,

POPCORN

or PLAY.

THESE... P words - are easier to say!

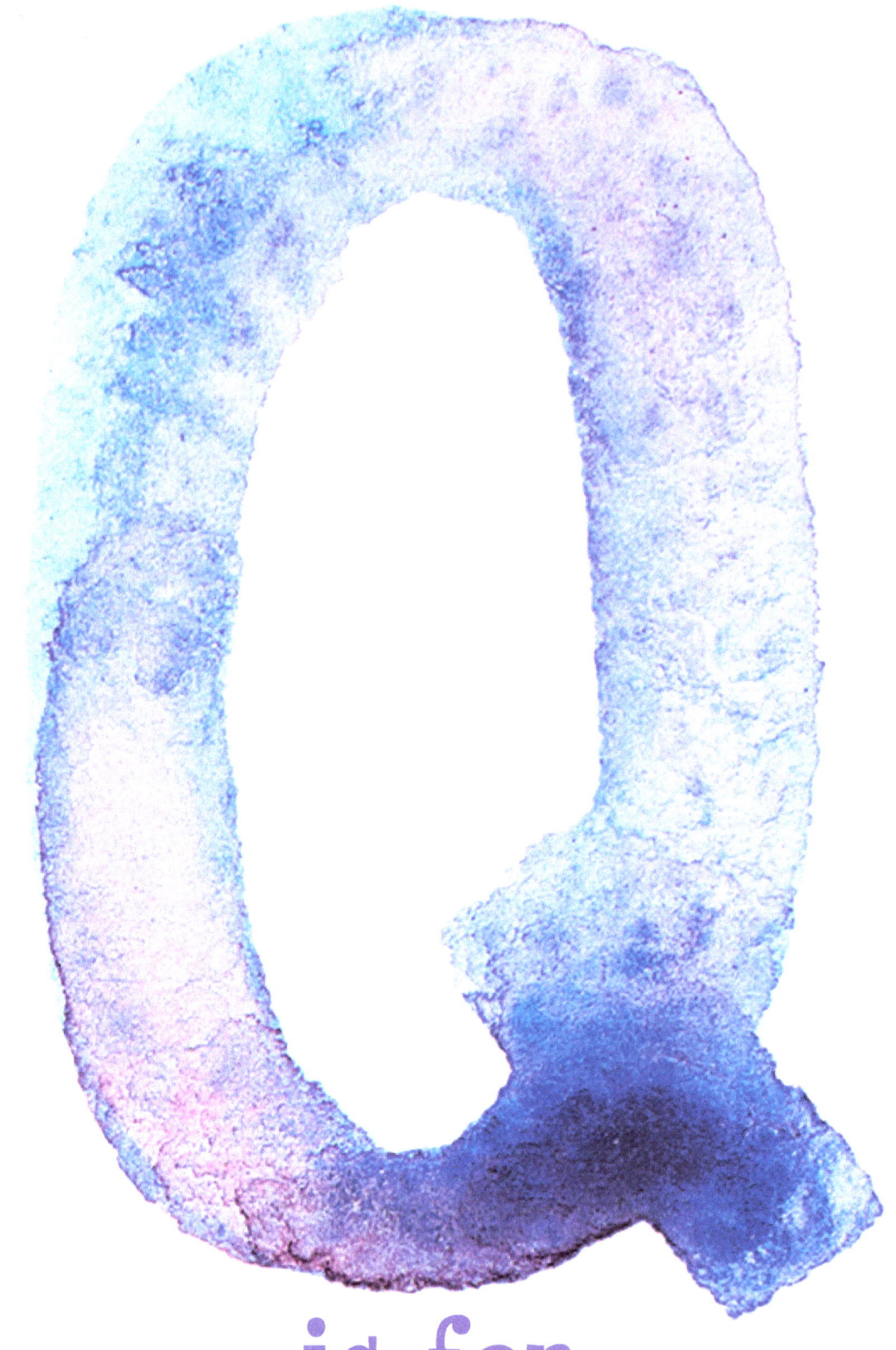

Q
is for
QUANTIFICATIONAL
kwon-tuh-fuh-*kay*-shu-nul

That which is able to be expressed in a quantity.

That might make you shudder.

So, QUEEN

and QUAIL are easier to utter.

So is QUARTER,

QUESTION

and QUILT.

But, QUANTIFICATIONAL...
could make your mind wilt!

R is for RECONCEPTUALIZATIONS

ree-kuhn-sep-choo-uh-lahy-zay-shuns

To, again, form into an idea or concept.

If that spins your head -

start with RICE

 or ROBOT

or RED.

And  is for RAT

and RABBIT

and RUN.

Learning R words - is fun, fun, fun!

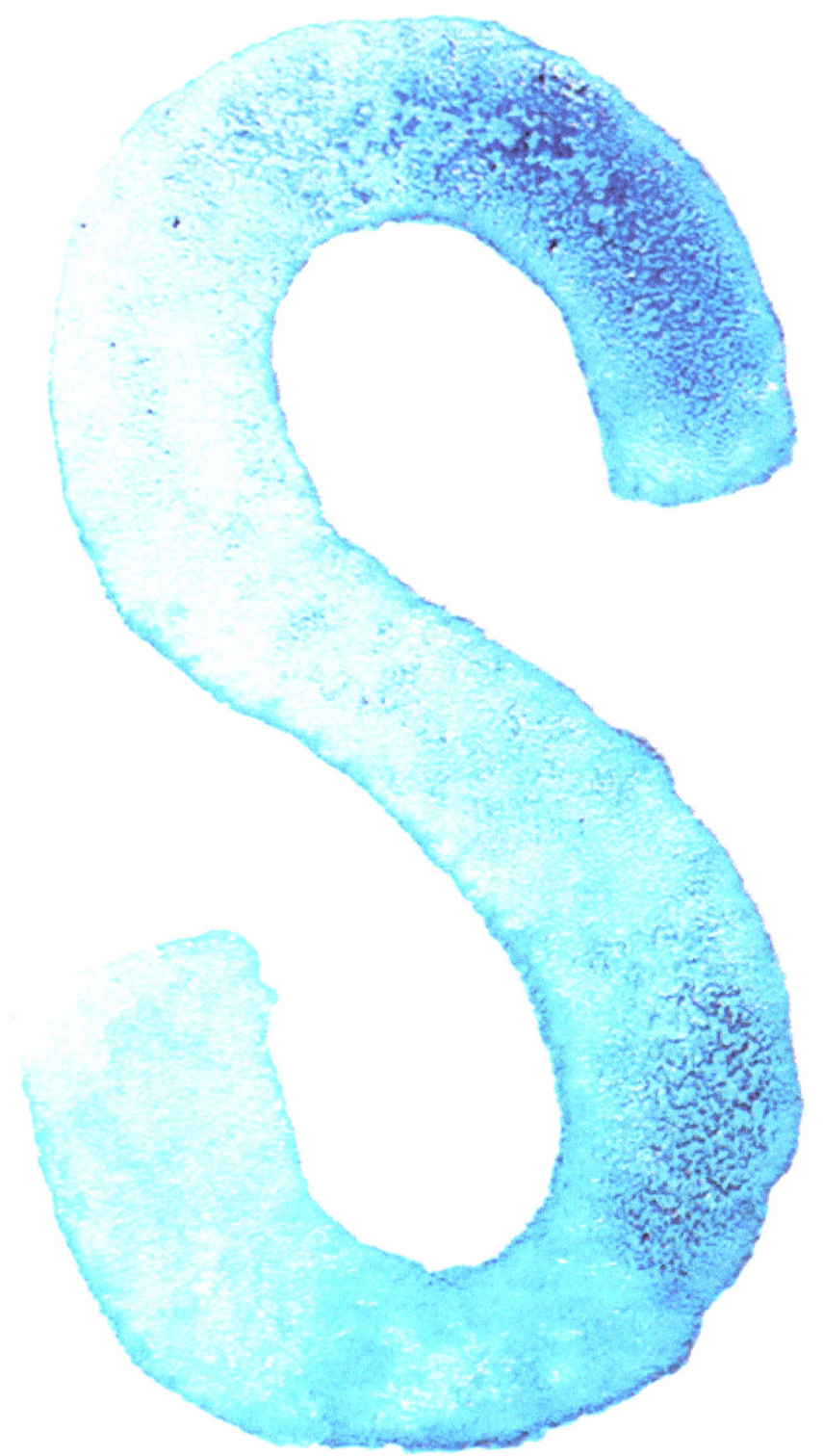

is for
SESQUIPEDALIANISM

ses-kwi-pi-**dey**-lee-uh-nism
The practice of using long, sometimes obscure, words.

Did you give it a try?

You could start with SUN

or STARS

or SKY.

Then move to SHIPS that SAIL the SEA.

Then end with SHIRT, SHOES or SKI!

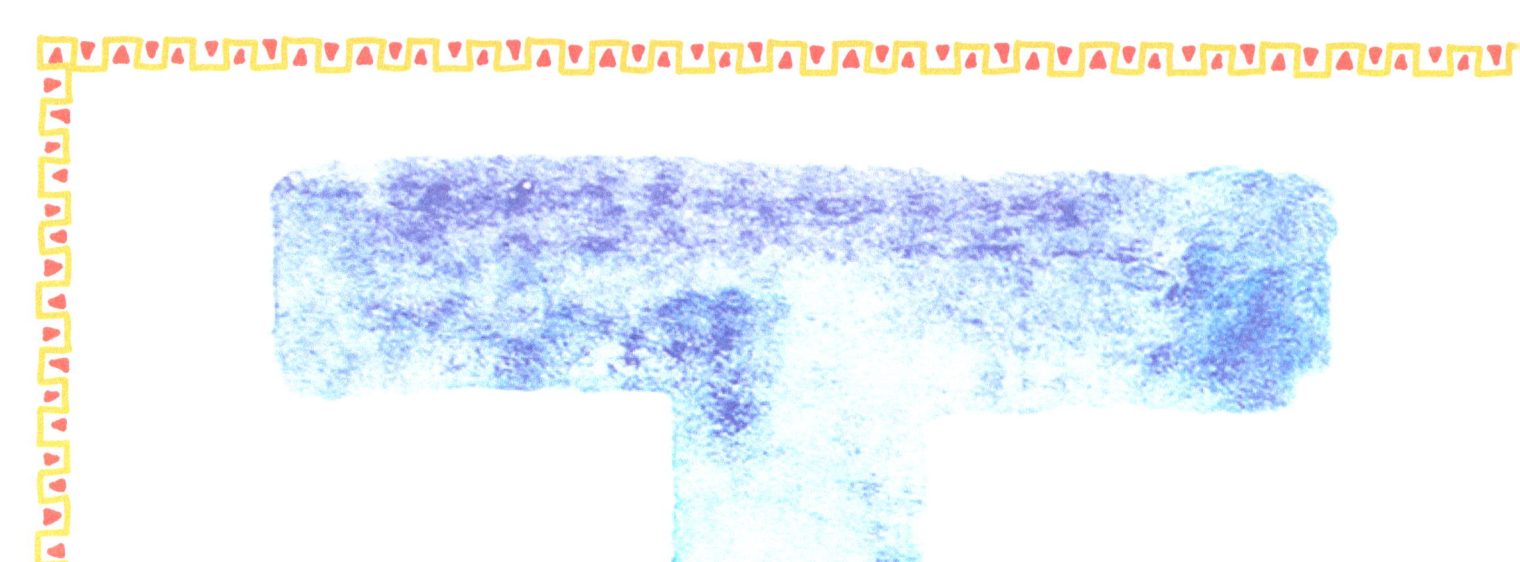

is for
TENDERHEARTEDNESS
ten-der-*hahr*-tid-nes
The characteristic of being caring and sympathetic.

It's a nice word to know.
But, if it's too long -
 you can start with TOE.

There's also TABLE,

TIGER and TREE.

TOAST  and TENT -

TURTLE  and TEA.

TRUCKS and TRAINS

both go TOOT!

Learning  words... is really a hoot!

U is for UNIMAGINATIVELY

un-ih-*maj*-uh-nuh-tiv-lee
Not done in a creative manner.

A word you can skip.

And start with UMBRELLA

or, maybe, UNZIP.

 is for UNCLE

and UNICORNS are fun.

There are many  words...

that start with UN.

V is for VULNERABILITIES

vuhl-ner-uh-**bihl**-i-tees
Specific weaknesses in the protection or defense of someone or something.

But, really, it's fine -

if you start with

VEGETABLE,

VAN

or VINE.

There's also **VIDEO**,

VILLAGE

 and VEST.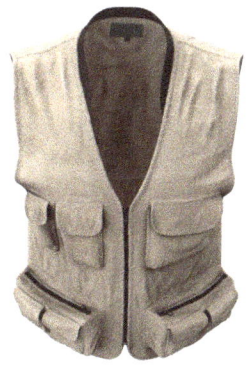

's a good letter - maybe the best?

W is for WARMHEARTEDNESS

wawrm-*hahr*-tid-nes
The quality of showing kindness, sympathy and affection.

Learn this! Please do!

While you're at it - learn

WHAT, **WHEN** and **WHO**.

There's **WATER**,

WALKING,

 **WAGON**

and **WINK**.

But, **WARMHEARTEDNESS** is **BEST** - that's what I think.

is for XYLOPHONIST

zahy-luh-*fohn*-ist

Someone who plays the xylophone.

But, a secret my friend.
X is rarely in **front** - it loves a words **END**.

Like SIX

and MIX

and WAX

and OX.

FIX

and FOX

and cardboard BOX.

Y is for YOUTHFULNESS

yooth-fuhl-nes
Done with or characterized by qualities of the young.

That rolls of the tongue.

So does YELLOW,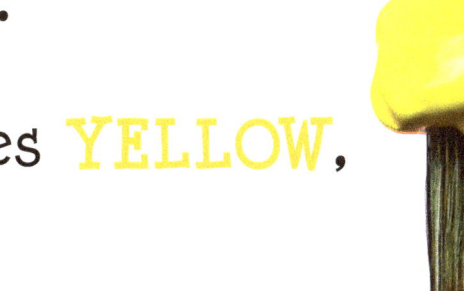

YOLK

and YOUNG.

And Y is for YEAR.

Y is for YUM.

There's one more letter - we're almost done.

Z is for ZEALOUSNESS

zel-uhs-nes

The quality of being full of eagerness, enthusiasm or zeal.

Z is also for ZONE.

Z is for ZUCCHINI -

did I hear you just moan?

There's also ZEBRA,

ZIPPERS

and ZOO.

From A to Z - *you made it through!*

Try our other children's books :

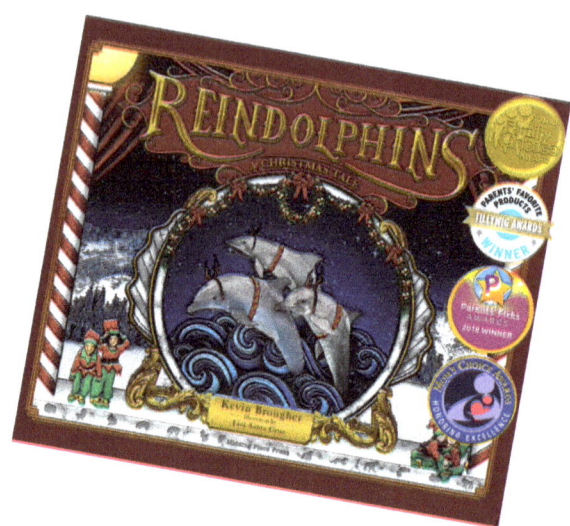

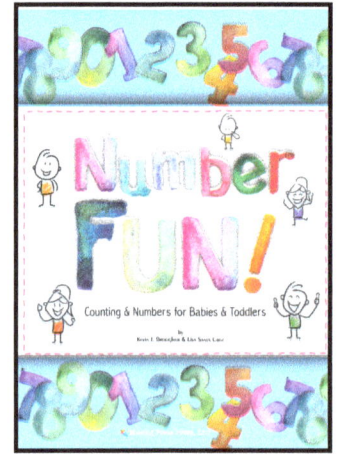

Visit **MissingPiecePress.com** to see our full line of award-winning **books** and **games**.

www.ingramcontent.com/pod-product-compliance
Lightning Source LLC
Chambersburg PA
CBHW061109070526
44579CB00012B/191